the rolling st
singles collection*
the london years

MW00804139

Alfred Music Publishing Co., Inc.
16320 Roscoe Blvd., Suite 100
P.O. Box 10003
Van Nuys, CA 91410-0003
alfred.com

ABKCO Music, Inc.
85 Fifth Avenue
New York, NY 10003
abkco.com

CONTENTS

AS TEARS GO BY

Words and Music by MICK JAGGER,
KEITH RICHARDS and ANDREW LOOG OLDHAM

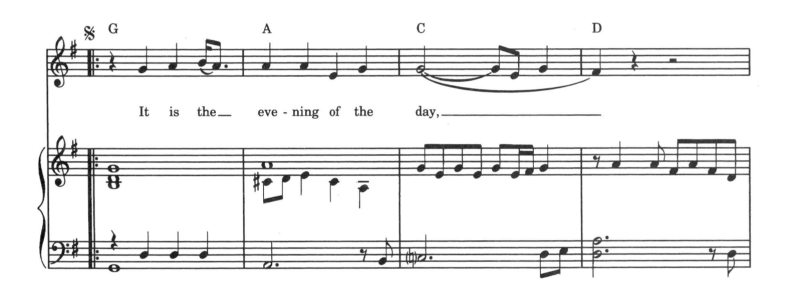

It is the__ eve-ning of the day,_____

I sit and__ watch the__ chil-dren play._____

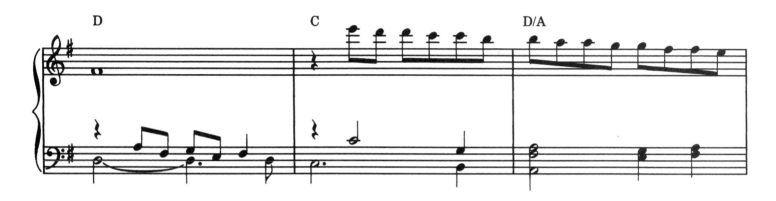

D.S. 𝄋 *and repeat to fade out (vocal hum)*

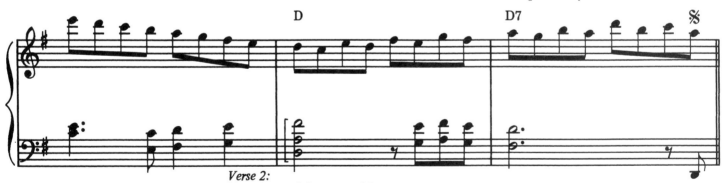

Verse 2:
My riches can't buy everything,
I want to hear the children sing.
All I hear is the sound of rain falling on the ground,
I sit and watch as tears go by.
To Instrumental:

Verse 3:
It is the evening of the day,
I sit and watch the children play.
Doin' things I used to do, they think are new,
I sit and watch as tears go by.
Mm mm mm. . .
To Instrumental and fade

BROWN SUGAR

Words and Music by
MICK JAGGER and KEITH RICHARDS

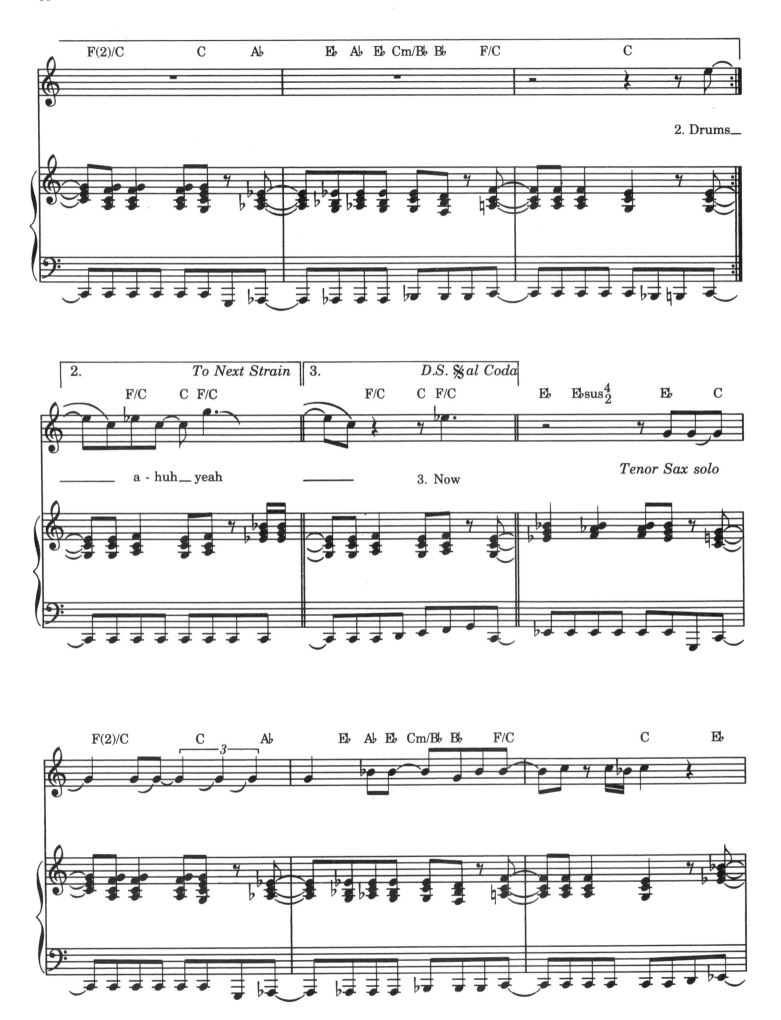

12

*Guitar & Tenor Sax blues riff - Tenor Sax plays lower harmony (♭3)

CHILD OF THE MOON

Words and Music by
MICK JAGGER and KEITH RICHARDS

Moderate rock ♩ = 104

1. The

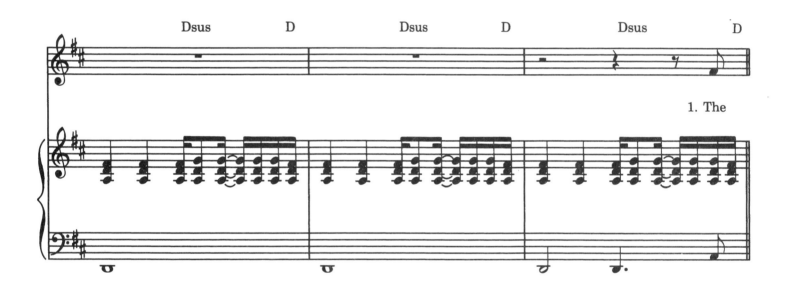

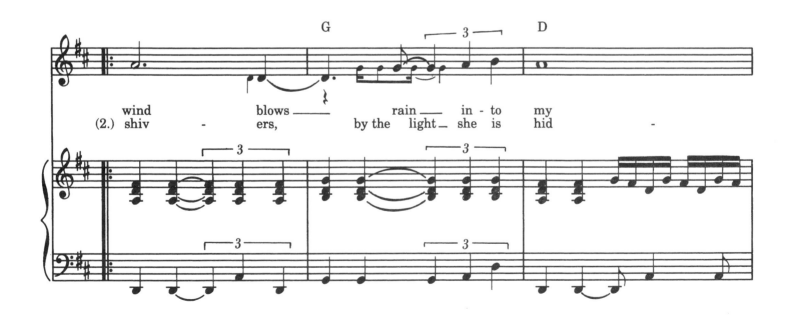

wind _____ blows _____ rain _____ in - to my
(2.) shiv - ers, by the light _ she is hid -

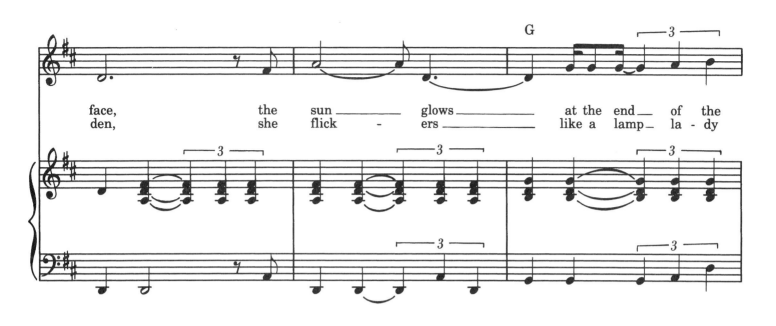

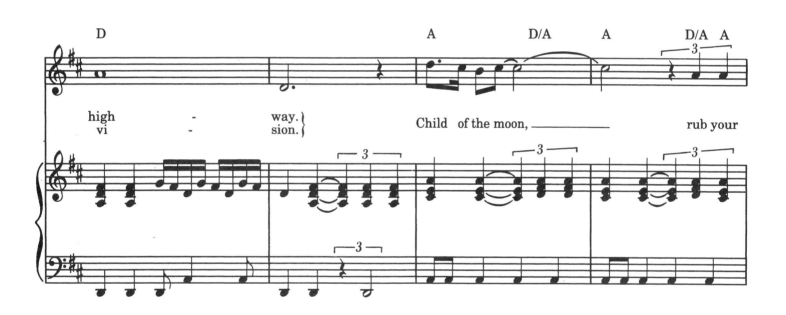

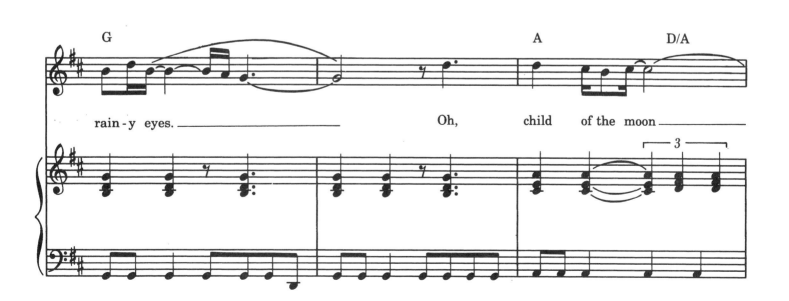

CONGRATULATIONS

Words and Music by
MICK JAGGER and KEITH RICHARDS

torn___ it a-part.___   *Guitar solo:*

Em   C   D   G   D7

___end solo

G   Em   G   Em

La, la,   la,   la, la, la, la, la, la.   La, la,   la,   la, la, la, la, la, la.

Repeat ad lib. and fade

C   D   G   D7

La, la, la, la,___ la,   la, la, la,   la___   ___   la,___ la, la, la, la, la.___

COME ON

Words and Music by
CHUCK BERRY

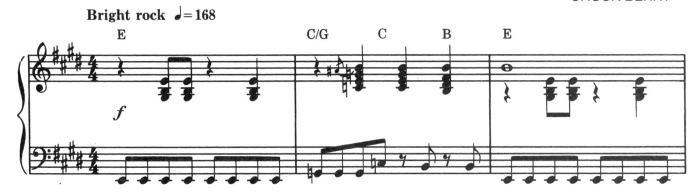

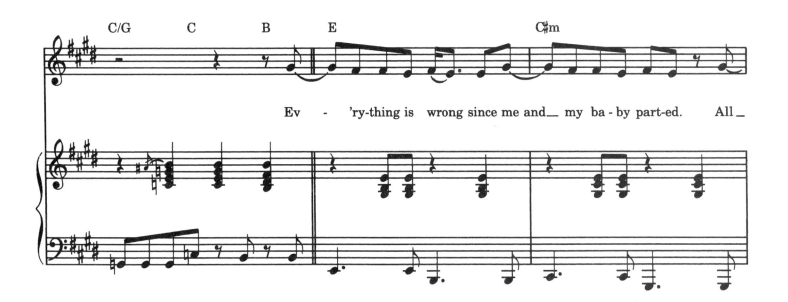

Ev - 'ry-thing is wrong since me and_ my ba - by part-ed. All _

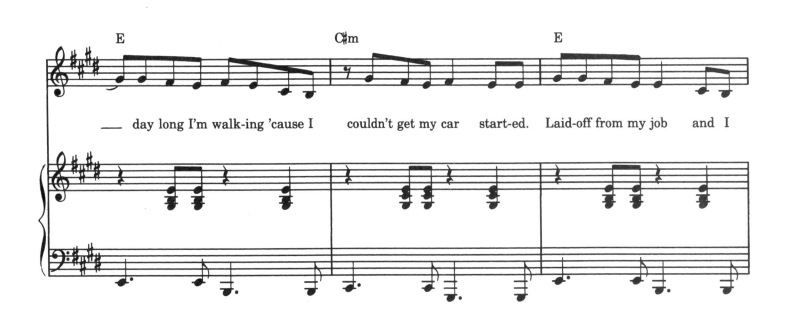

_ day long I'm walk-ing 'cause I couldn't get my car start-ed. Laid-off from my job and I

try'n' to make you see }
got - ta make you see }
that I be-long to you and you be-long to me. Come on,

Come on!
Come

on!
Come on!

DANDELION

Words and Music by
MICK JAGGER and KEITH RICHARDS

I DON'T KNOW WHY

Words and Music by STEVIE WONDER,
LULA MAE HARDAWAY, PAUL RISER
and DON HUNTER

I___ love you, babe..

Verse 2 & 3:

2. 3. When are you gon-na stop your___ cheat-in'___ ways___ with

an-oth-er guy,— you__ laugh__ in my face._____

Just how long__ must I be_____ dis - graced__ 'cause I

I love__ you ba - by?__ uh - huh. *I tell ya'*

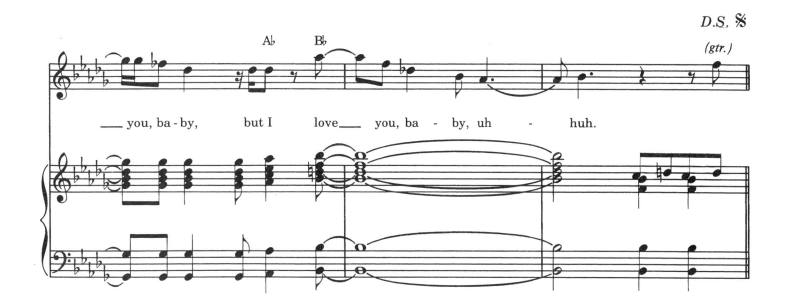

GOOD TIMES, BAD TIMES

Words and Music by
MICK JAGGER and KEITH RICHARDS

Repeat ad lib. and fade

GOTTA GET AWAY

Words and Music by
MICK JAGGER and KEITH RICHARDS

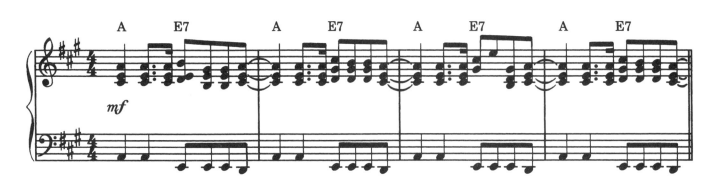

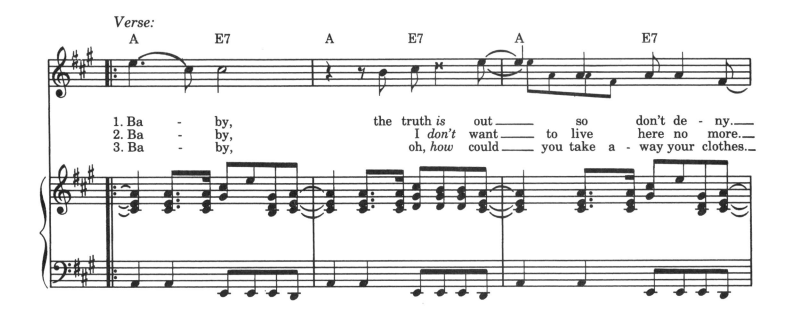

GET OFF OF MY CLOUD

Words and Music by
MICK JAGGER and KEITH RICHARDS

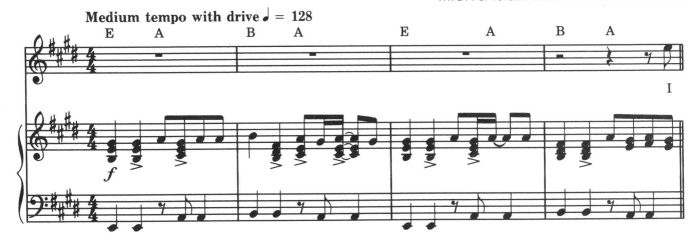

live in — an a-part-ment on — the nine - ty-ninth floor — of my block, —

and I sit at home look-ing out — the win-dow, im - ag-in-ing — the world has stopped.

Verse 2:
The telephone is ringing, I say, "Hi, it's me, Who is it there on the line?"
A voice says, "Hi, hello, how are you?" Well, I guess I'm doin' fine.
He says, "It's three a.m., there's too much noise. Don't you people ever wanna go to bed?
Just 'cause you feel so good, do you have to drive me out of my head?"
To Chorus:

Verse 3:
I was sick and tired, fed up with this, and decided to take a drive downtown.
It was so very quiet and peaceful, there was nobody, not a soul around.
I laid myself out, I was so tired, and I started to dream.
In the morning the parking tickets were just like a flag stuck on my window screen.
To Chorus:

HEART OF STONE

Words and Music by
MICK JAGGER and KEITH RICHARDS

Moderately slow ballad ♩. = 64

1. There have been so

man- y ___ girls that I've known.

I've made so man-y cry and still I won-der why.

Here comes the lit-tle girl, I see her walk-ing down the street._

She's all_ by_ her-self I try and knock her off her feet. { But she'll } { 'Cause you'll }

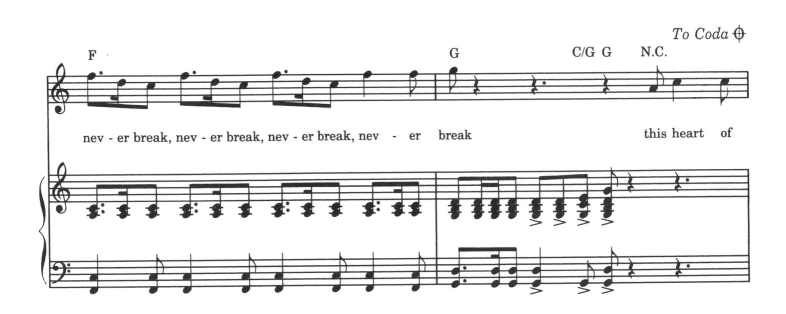

To Coda ⊕

nev - er break, nev - er break, nev - er break, nev - er break this heart of

*8va if played by guitar

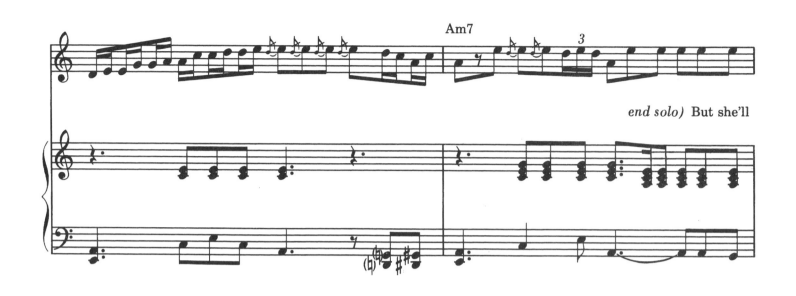

end solo) But she'll

nev - er break, nev - er break, nev - er break, nev - er break   this heart   of

D.S. %al Coda

stone.   Oh, no,   no, no. This heart of ___ stone. ___   2. Don't keep on

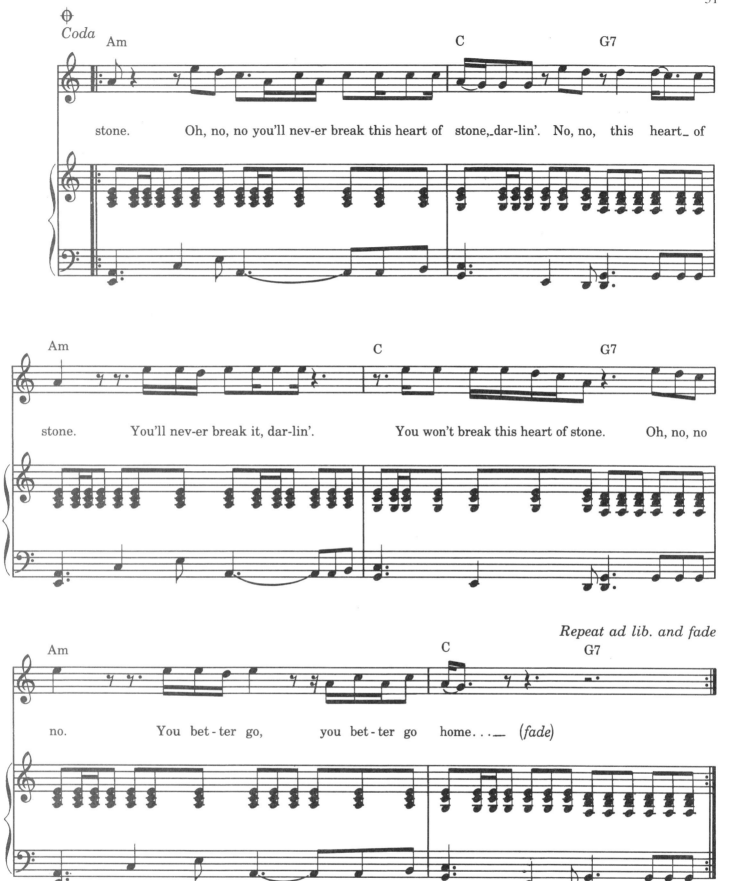

Verse 2:
Don't keep on looking that same old way.
If you try acting sad, you'll only make me glad.
Better listen little girl,
You go on walking down the street.
I ain't got no love, I ain't the kind to meet.

HAVE YOU SEEN YOUR MOTHER, BABY, STANDING IN THE SHADOW?

Words and Music by
MICK JAGGER and KEITH RICHARDS

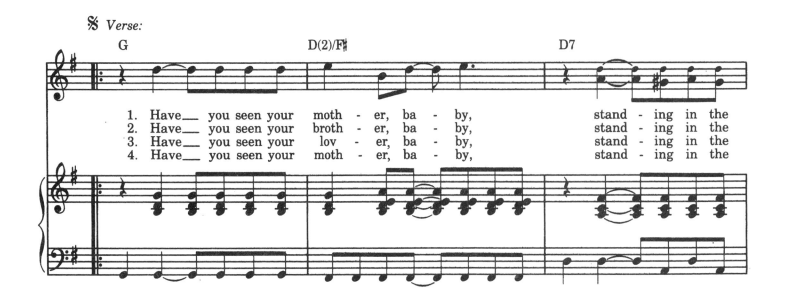

1. Have____ you seen your moth - er, ba - by, stand - ing in the
2. Have____ you seen your broth - er, ba - by, stand - ing in the
3. Have____ you seen your lov - er, ba - by, stand - ing in the
4. Have____ you seen your moth - er, ba - by, stand - ing in the

HONKY TONK WOMEN

Words and Music by
MICK JAGGER and KEITH RICHARDS

Rock ♩ = 115

Verse:

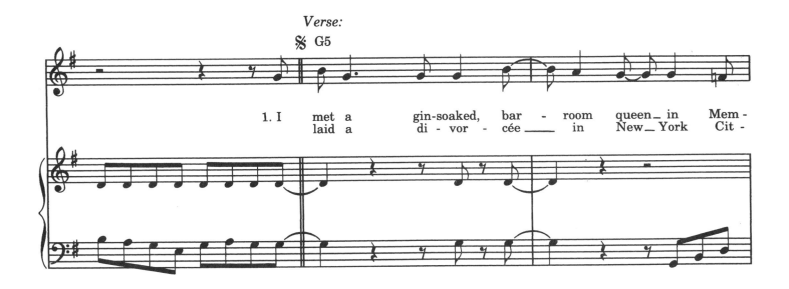

1. I met a gin-soaked, bar-room queen in Mem-
laid a di-vor-cée in New York Cit-

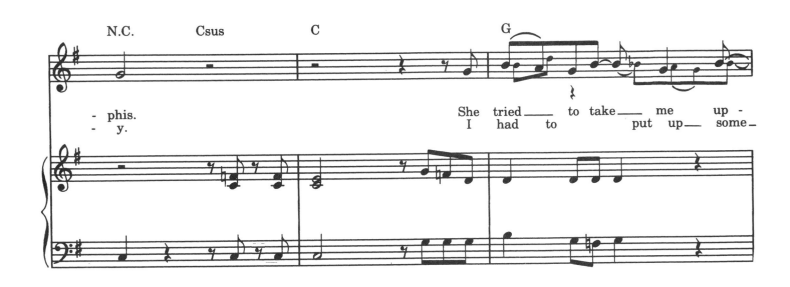

-phis.   She tried to take me up-
-y.   I had to put up some-

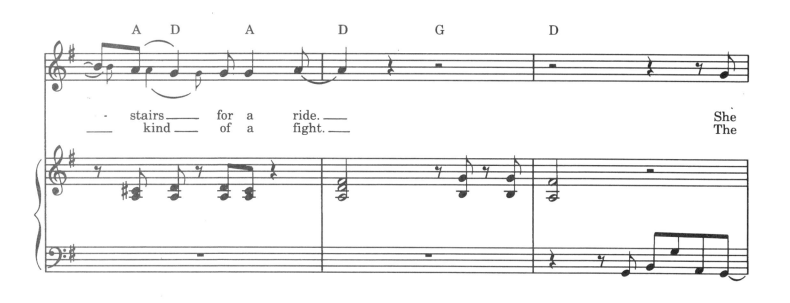

stairs_____ for a ride._____
kind_____ of a fight._____

She
The

had to heave me right_____ a - cross___her shoul - der,
la - dy then she cov - ered me ___ in ros - es,

1.

'cause I just can't seem to drink you off my___ mind.___

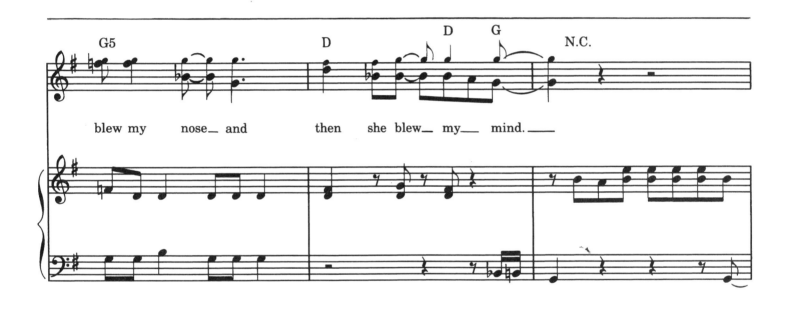

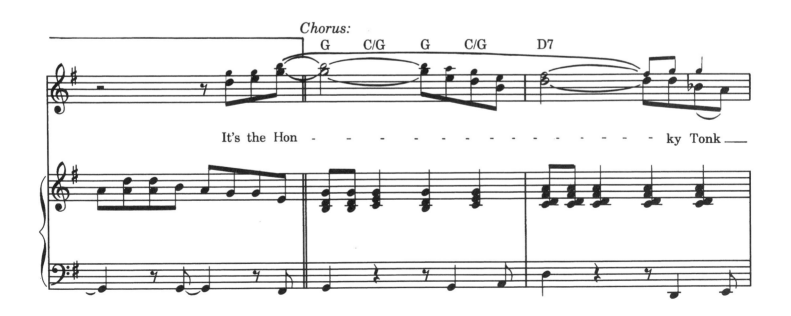

*8va if played by guitar

...*solo ends*   It's the Hon -

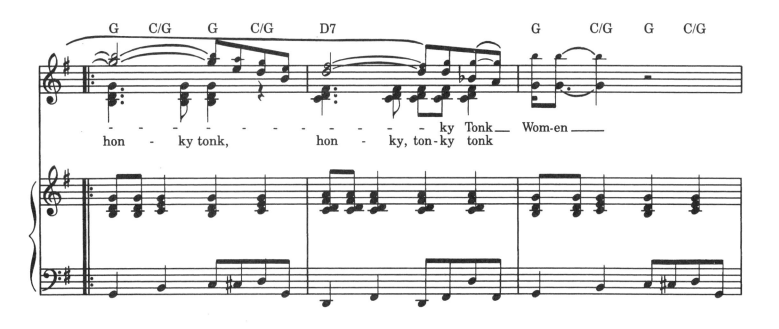

I JUST WANT TO MAKE LOVE TO YOU

Words and Music by
WILLIE DIXON

sad and blue.⎫
mon-ey too. ⎬ I just want to make love to you, ba - by,
sad and blue.⎭

(Gtr.)

To Coda ⊕ │1.

love to you ba-by, love to you ba-by, love to you.

│2.

C

you. Well, I can tell by the way that you that__ walk.__ See by the

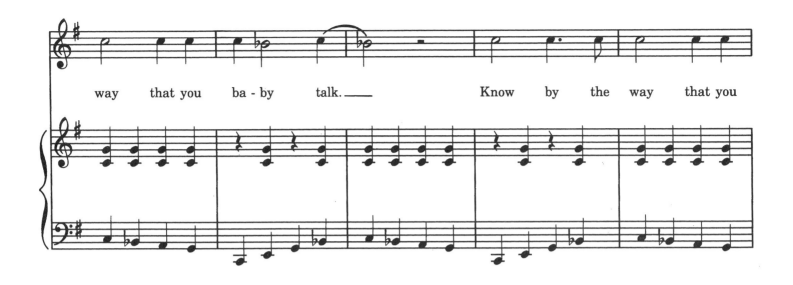

way   that you   ba - by   talk.____   Know   by   the   way   that you

D.S. 𝄋 al Coda

D

treat your   man.____   I can   love   ya,____   ba - by, 'til the   light   change.____

Coda

C

D

(6 times)

(Gtr.)

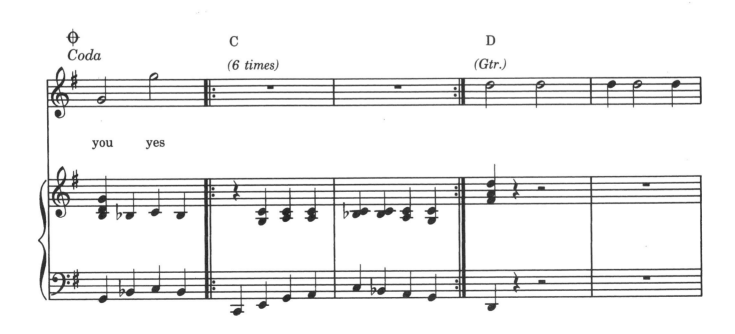

you   yes

I WANNA BE YOUR MAN

Words and Music by
JOHN LENNON and PAUL McCARTNEY

1. I wan-na be your lov-er ba-by, I wan-na be your man.
2. Tell me that you love me ba-by, tell me you un-der-stand.

I wan-na be your lov-er ba-by, I wan-na be your man.___
Tell me that you love me ba-by, tell me you un-der-stand.___

Chorus:

(gtr)

I wan-na be your man.___

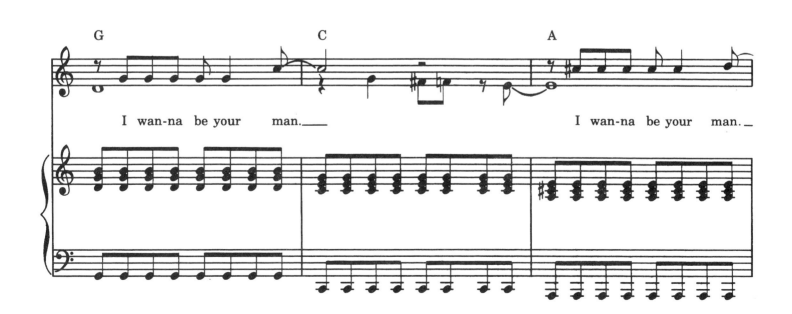

I wan-na be your man.___

I wan-na be your man.___

I wan-na be your man.___

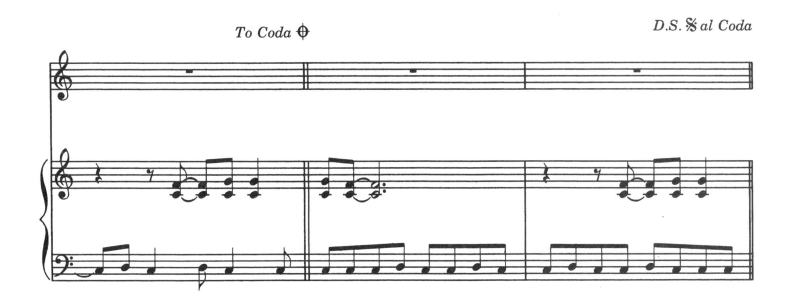

To Coda ⊕

D.S. 𝄋 *al Coda*

⊕
Coda   C

Tell   me   that   you   love me,   ba - by.
I   wan - na   be   your   lov - er,   ba - by.

I WANNA BE LOVED

Words and Music by
WILLIE DIXON

I'M FREE

Words and Music by
MICK JAGGER and KEITH RICHARDS

*Harmony vocal 8va.

*Harmony vocal 8va.
**8va if played by guitar.

Verse 3:
I'm free to choose what I please any old time.
I'm free to please who I choose and old time.
To Chorus:

IN ANOTHER LAND

Words and Music by
BILL WYMAN

grass grew high and the feath-ers float-ed by I stood and held your
spray flew high and the feath-ers float-ed by I stood and held your
came to be here not fast a-sleep in bed. I stood and held your

Chorus

hand.
hand.
hand.

1. 2. And no-bod-y else'-s hand will ev-er do
3. And no-bod-y else'-s hand will ev-er do

no-bod-y else will do. Then I a-woke
no-bod-y else'-s hand. Then I a-woke

IT'S ALL OVER NOW

Words and Music by
BOBBY and SHIRLEY WOMACK

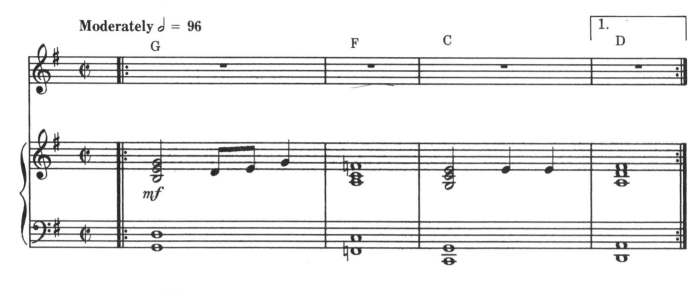

84

D. S. % al Coda

-stead of trying to take me for that same old___ clown. Be-cause I

Coda

Be-cause I used to___ love her, but it's all___ o - ver now.___

Repeat ad lib. and fade

JIVING SISTER FANNY

Words and Music by
MICK JAGGER and KEITH RICHARDS

JUMPIN' JACK FLASH

Words and Music by
MICK JAGGER and KEITH RICHARDS

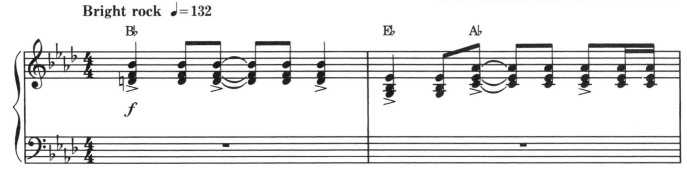

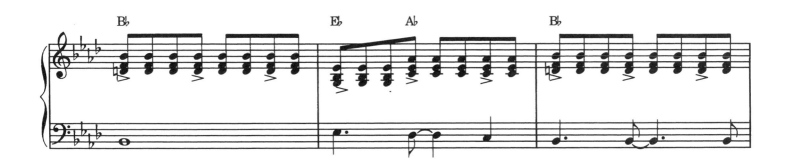

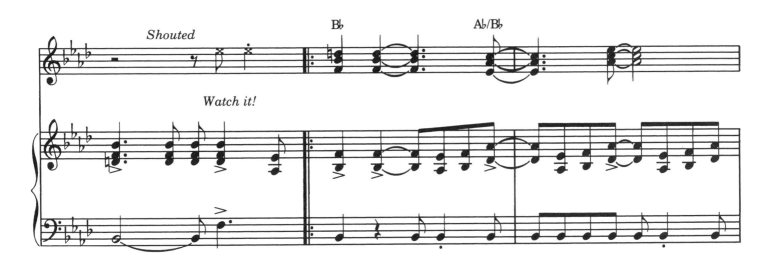

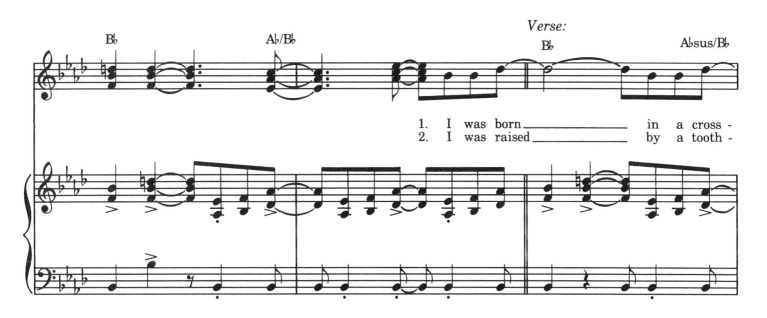

Verse:

1. I was born_____ in a cross -
2. I was raised_____ by a tooth -

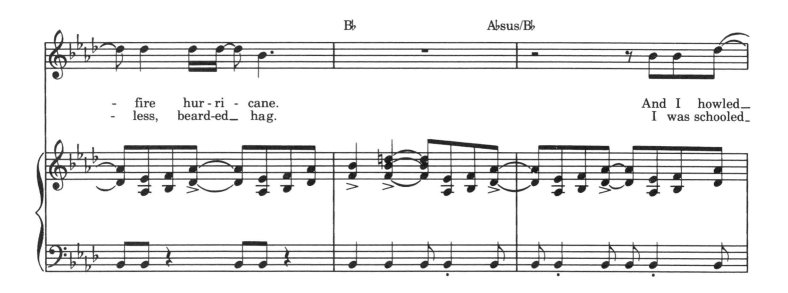

- fire   hur - ri - cane.   And I howled__
- less, beard-ed__ hag.   I was schooled__

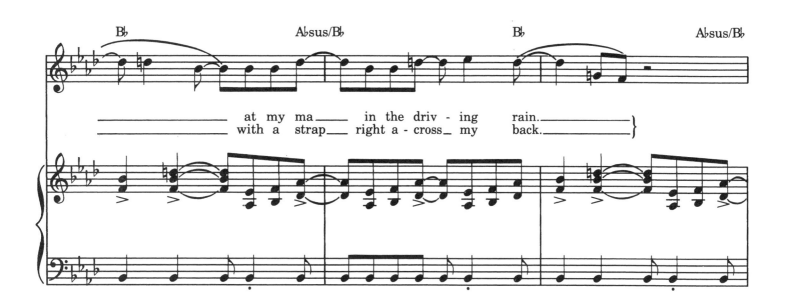

_____ at my ma_____ in the driv - ing   rain._____
_____ with a strap___ right a - cross__ my back._____ }

* 8va if played by Guitar.

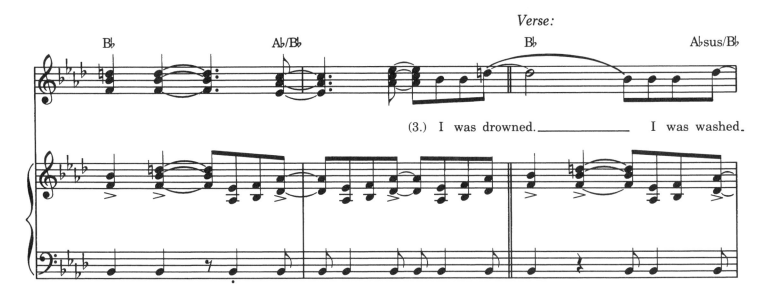

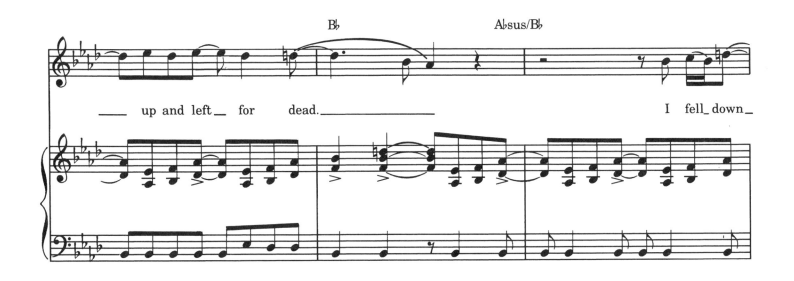

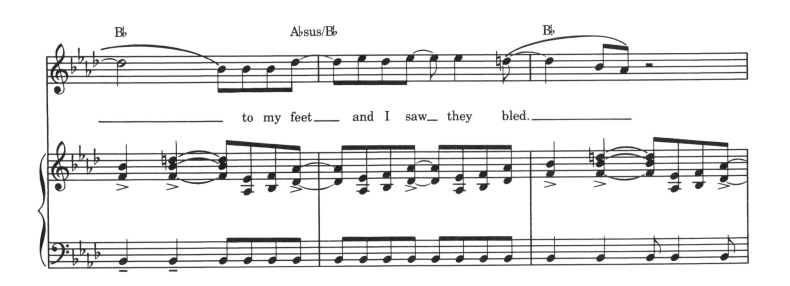

I frowned _____ at the crumbs_ of a crust_ of bread._

_____ I was crowned _____ with a spike__

D.S. 𝄋 al Coda

___ right through my_ head._____ But it's all__

Coda

Play 4 times

Jump-in' Jack Flash, it's a gas!__ Jump-in' Jack Flash,

Organ

it's a gas!__

LADY JANE

Words and Music by
MICK JAGGER and KEITH RICHARDS

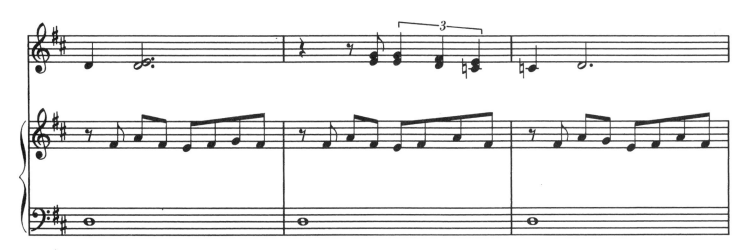

*8va if played by guitar.

and will hum - bly   re - main.__
for prom-ised   I   am.__
for your la - dy   and   me.__

Bridge:

Just   heed   this   plea,   my   love.
This   play   is   run,   my   love.
When   love   is   nigh,   my   love,

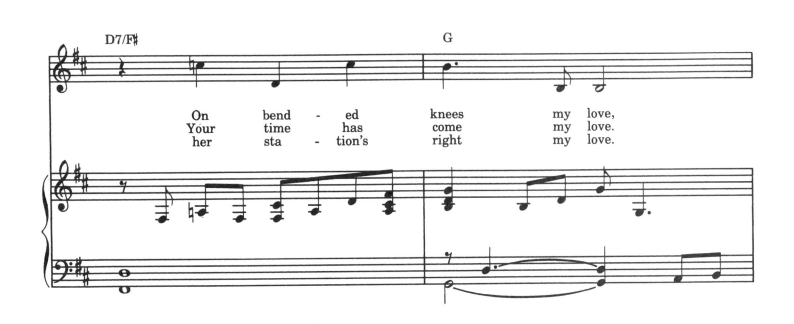

On   bend - ed   knees   my   love,
Your   time   has   come   my   love.
her   sta - tion's   right   my   love.

THE LANTERN

Words and Music by
MICK JAGGER and KEITH RICHARDS

*8va if played by guitar.

LITTLE BY LITTLE

Words and Music by
NANKER PHELGE and PHIL SPECTOR

THE LAST TIME

Words and Music by
MICK JAGGER and KEITH RICHARDS

(Guitar solo)*

Vocal: Well, this could be the

*8va if played by guitar

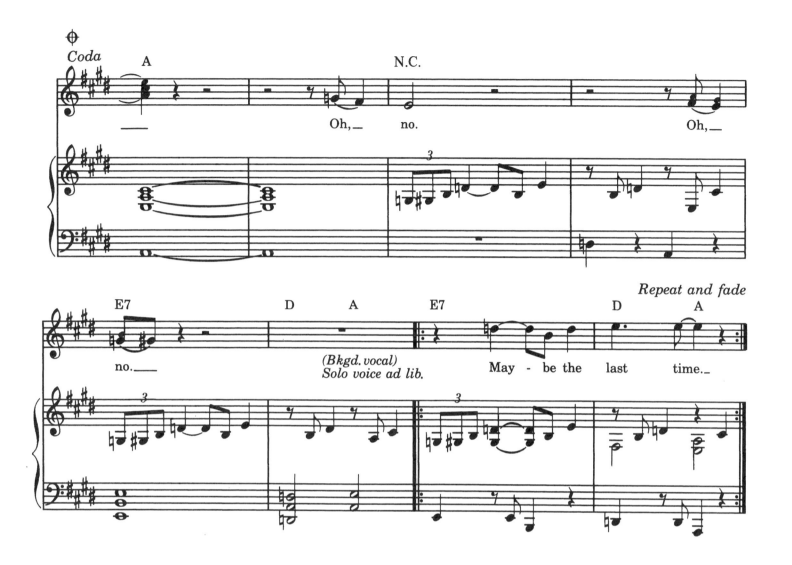

Well, I'm sorry, girl, but I can't stay,
Feelin' like I do today.
It's too much pain and too much sorrow;
Guess I'll feel the same tomorrow.
(To Chorus:)

Verse 3:
Well, I told you once and I told you twice;
That someone will have to pay the price,
But, here's a chance to change your mind,
'Cuz I'll be gone a long, long time.
(To Chorus:)

LET'S SPEND THE NIGHT TOGETHER

Words and Music by
MICK JAGGER and KEITH RICHARDS

* Play Bm 2nd & 3rd times.

LITTLE RED ROOSTER

Words and Music by
WILLIE DIXON

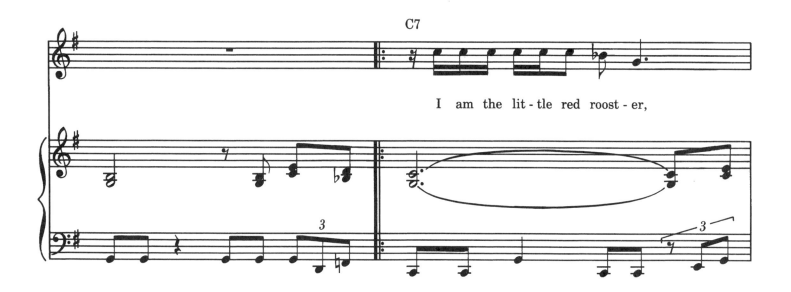

I am the lit - tle red roost - er,

too la - zy to crow to-day.

Keep ev-'ry-thing in the farm - yard,

Up - set — in ev-'ry way. —

The dogs be-gin to bark-in', hounds be-gin to howl. —

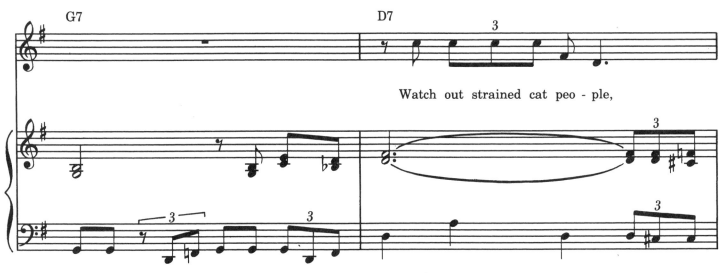

Watch out strained cat peo - ple,

Lit-tle red roost-er's on the prowl.

If you see my lit-tle red roost-er,   please ___ drive him home.

Ain't had no peace in the farm - yard,   since my lit-tle red roost-er's been gone.

Harmonica: *Repeat and fade*

LONG LONG WHILE

Words and Music by
MICK JAGGER and KEITH RICHARDS

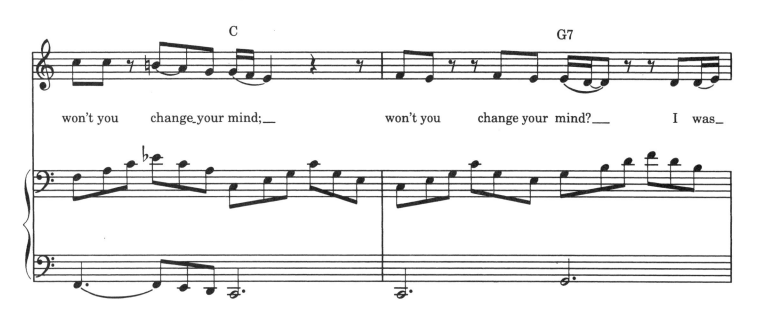

MEMO FROM TURNER

Words and Music by
MICK JAGGER and KEITH RICHARDS

Aw, you drowned / that Jew in Rampton / as he washed his sleeveless
- tised. You're the / great, gray man whose / daughter licks po -

shirt.
- licemen's buttons / clean. You're the / man who squats be -

You know, that Spanish-speaking / gentleman, the

one that we all called / "Kurt." Sung: Come now,
- hind the man who works / the soft ma - chine. Come now,

MOTHER'S LITTLE HELPER

Words and Music by
MICK JAGGER and KEITH RICHARDS

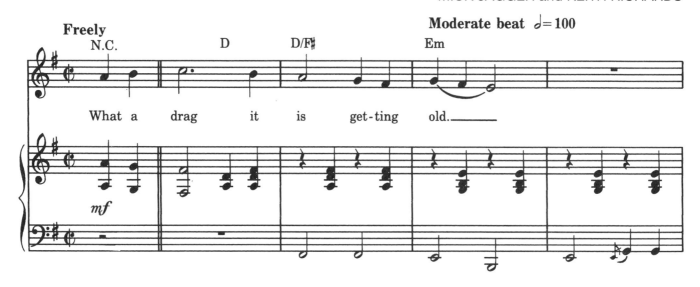

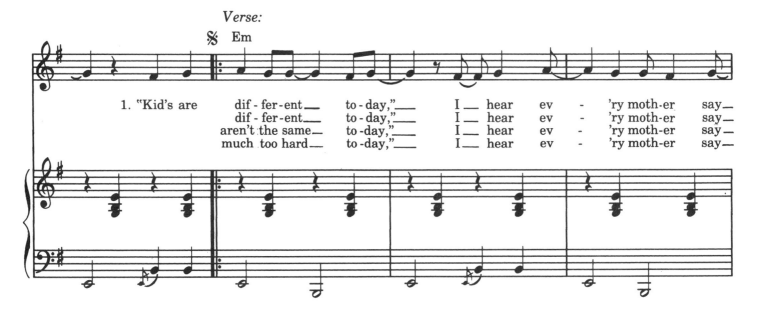

- er and it helps her on her way, __ gets her through __ her bus-y day. _
- er and two help her on her way, __ get her through __ her bus-y day. _
- er and four help you through the night, _ help to min-i - mize _ your plight. _
- er they just helped you on your way __ through your bus-y dy - ing day. _

To Coda ⊕

Instrumental

1.

2. 3.

Chorus:

C

__ 2. "Things are __ Doc - tor please _____ some more _ of these _

19TH NERVOUS BREAKDOWN

Words and Music by
MICK JAGGER and KEITH RICHARDS

Fast Rock ♩ = 192

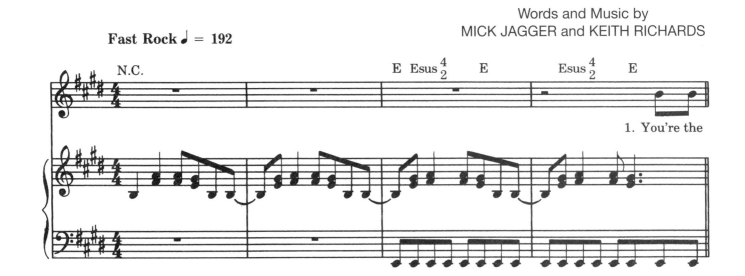

1. You're the

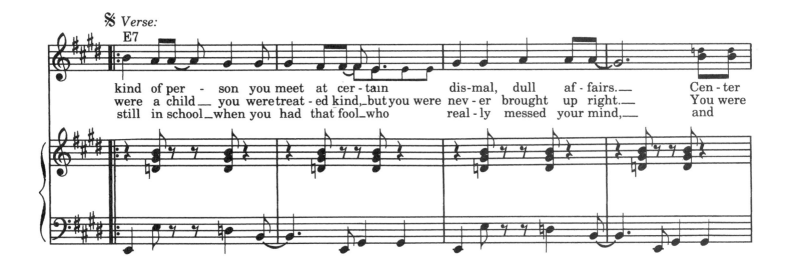

kind of per - son you meet at cer - tain dis-mal, dull af - fairs.__ Cen - ter
were a child__ you were treat - ed kind, but you were nev - er brought up right.__ You were
still in school__ when you had that fool__ who real - ly messed your mind,__ and

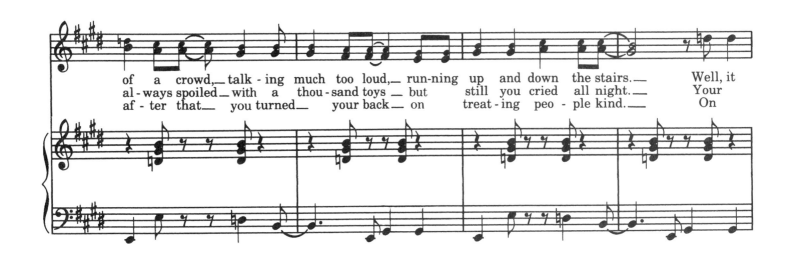

of a crowd,__ talk - ing much too loud,__ run-ning up and down the stairs.__ Well, it
al - ways spoiled__ with a thou-sand toys__ but still you cried all night.__ Your
af - ter that__ you turned__ your back__ on treat - ing peo - ple kind.__ On

Oh, who's to ___ blame, ___ that

girl's just in - sane. ___ Well,

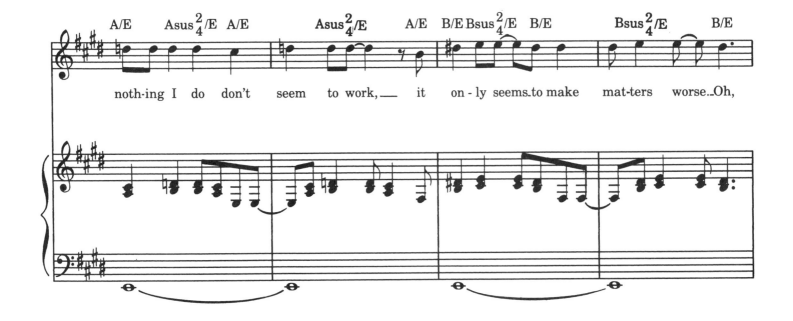

noth-ing I do don't seem to work, ___ it on - ly seems to make mat-ters worse. Oh,

NOT FADE AWAY

Words and Music by
CHARLES HARDIN and NORMAN PETTY

I want to tell you how it's gon-na be.
My love's big-ger than a Cad - il - lac.
I'm gon-na tell you how it's gon - na be.

You're gon-na give your love to me.
I try to show it then you drive me back.
You're gon-na give your love to me.

Well, love a-real_and not fade a-way.__

Harmonica

D. S. 𝄋 al Coda

NO EXPECTATIONS

Words and Music by
MICK JAGGER and KEITH RICHARDS

(acoustic slide guitar)

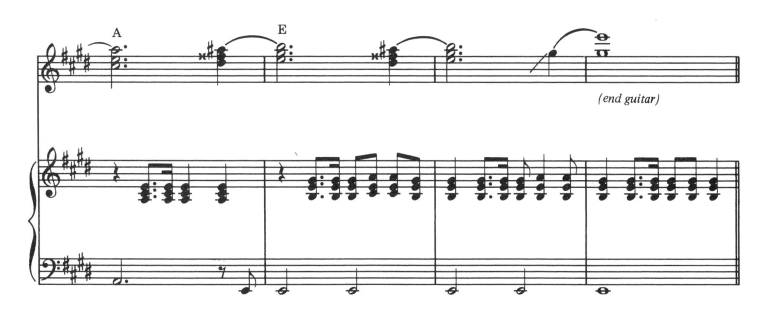

(end guitar)

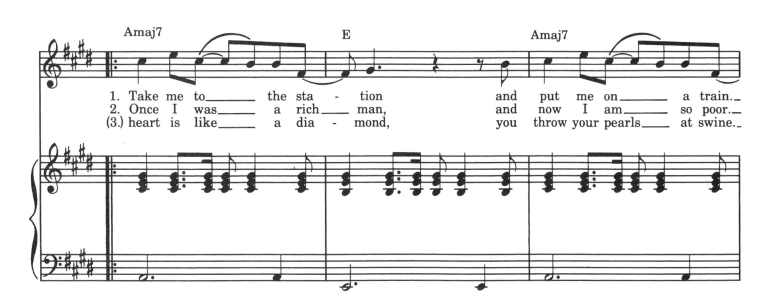

1. Take me to_____ the sta - tion   and put me on_____ a train._
2. Once I was_____ a rich_____ man,   and now I am_____ so poor._
(3.) heart is like_____ a dia - mond,   you throw your pearls_____ at swine._

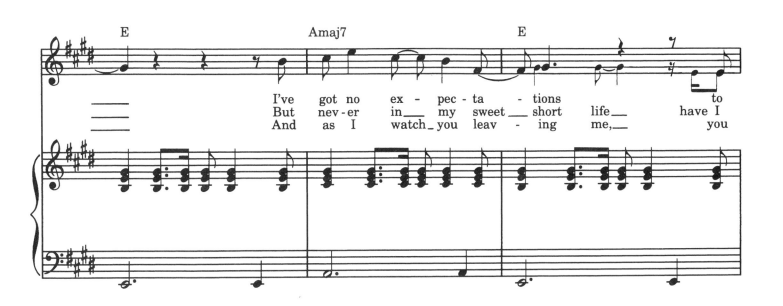

_____   I've got no ex - pec - ta - tions   to
_____   But nev - er in__ my sweet __ short life__ have I
_____   And as I watch__ you leav - ing me,__ you

pass / felt / pack
through here / like this / my peace
a - gain. / be - fore. / of mind.

(slide guitar)

D   A   E   A/E

E   A/E   1. E   2. E   3. E

(... end guitar)   (... end guitar)   3. Your

Amaj7   E   Amaj7   E   Amaj7

E   D   A   E

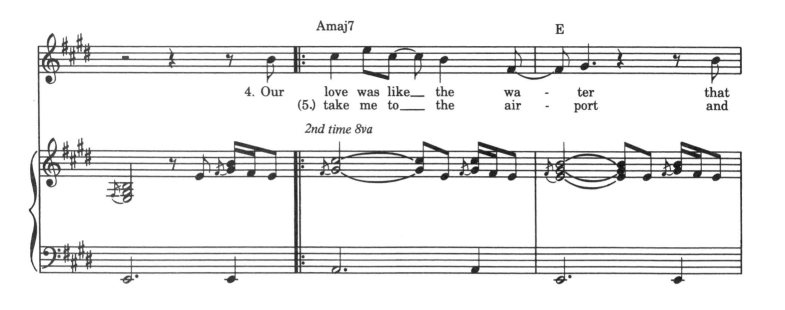

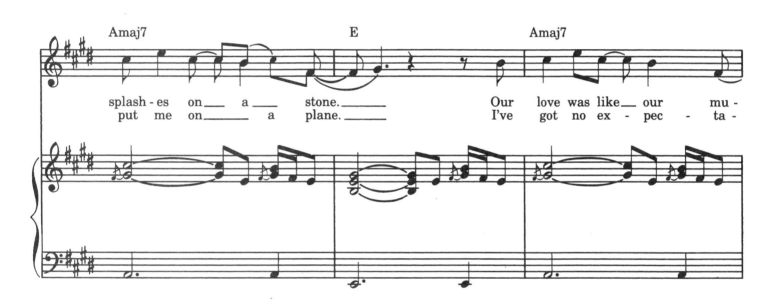

OFF THE HOOK

Words and Music by
MICK JAGGER and KEITH RICHARDS

*8va if played by Guitar.

OUT OF TIME

Words and Music by
MICK JAGGER and KEITH RICHARDS

PAINT IT, BLACK

Words and Music by
MICK JAGGER and KEITH RICHARDS

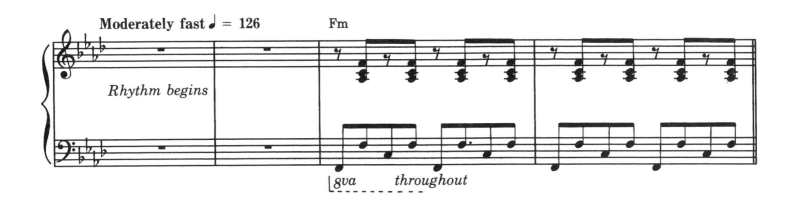

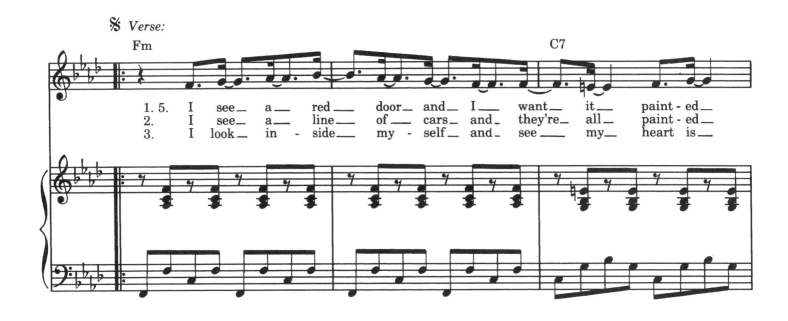

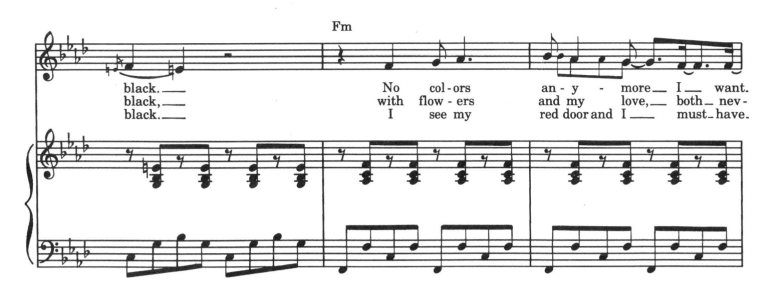

black.____ No col-ors an - y - more__ I __ want.
black,____ with flow - ers and my love,__ both__ nev -
black.____ I see my red door and I ____ must_have.

Bridge:

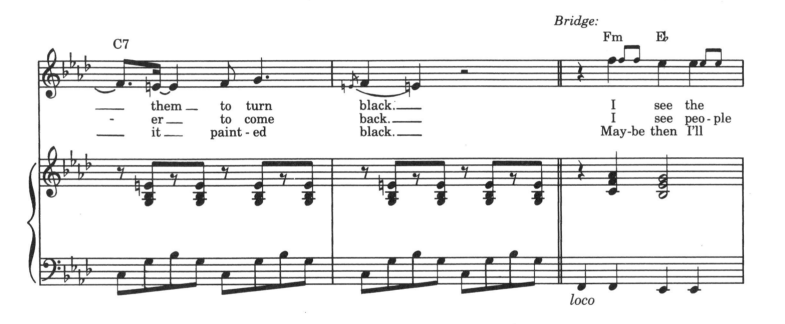

____ them __ to turn black.____ I see the
- er __ to come back.____ I see peo - ple
____ it __ paint - ed black.____ May-be then I'll

loco

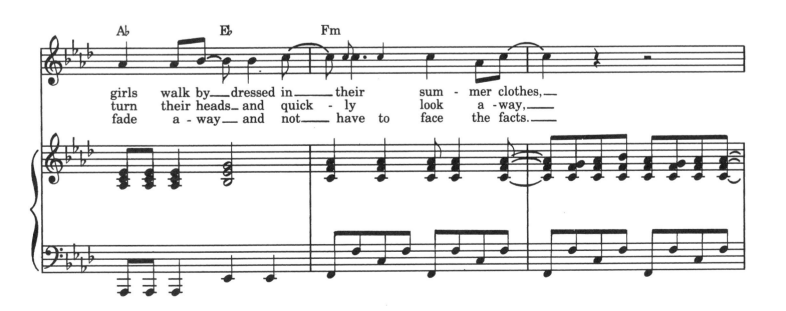

girls walk by__dressed in__their sum - mer clothes,__
turn their heads__ and quick - ly look a - way,__
fade a - way__ and not__have to face the facts.__

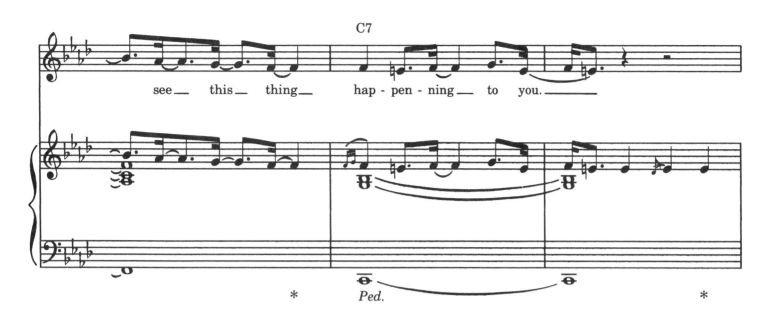

see___ this___ thing___ hap - pen - ning ___ to you.___

Bridge:

If I look hard e - nough in - to___ the___ set - ting sun,___

D. S. 𝄋 al Coda

my love will laugh with me___ be - fore___ the morn - ing comes. ___

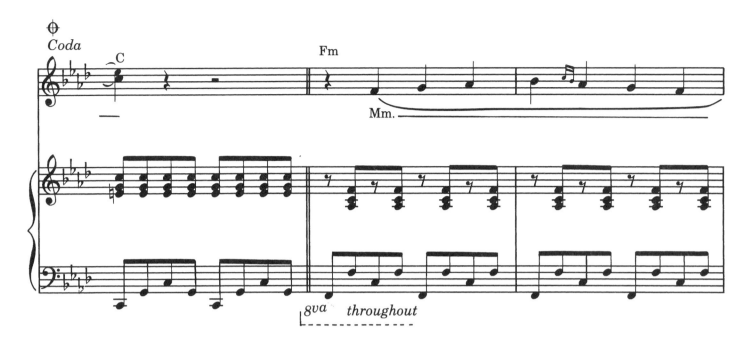

PLAY WITH FIRE

Words and Music by
MICK JAGGER and KEITH RICHARDS

Verse 1:

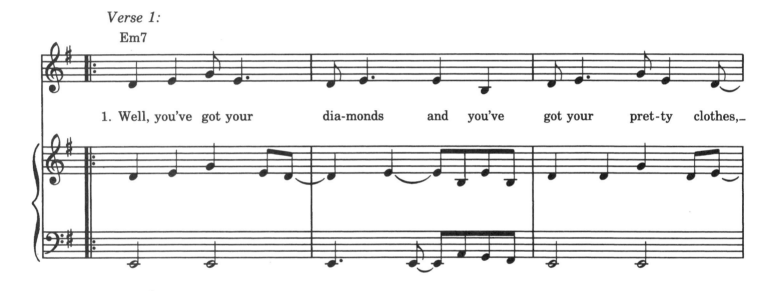

1. Well, you've got your dia-monds and you've got your pret-ty clothes,____

____ and the chauf-feur drives your car,____ you let

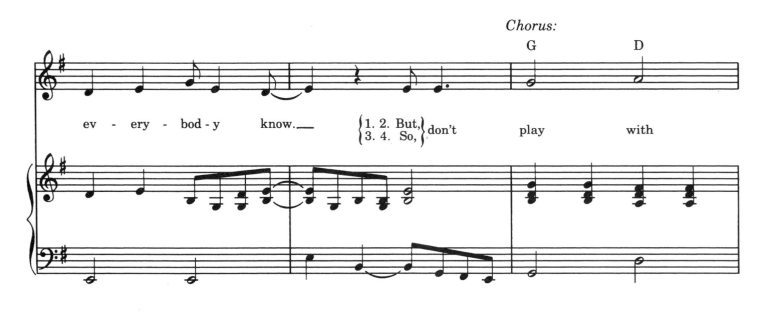

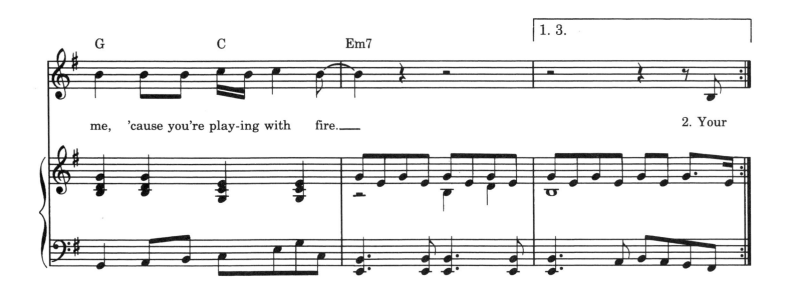

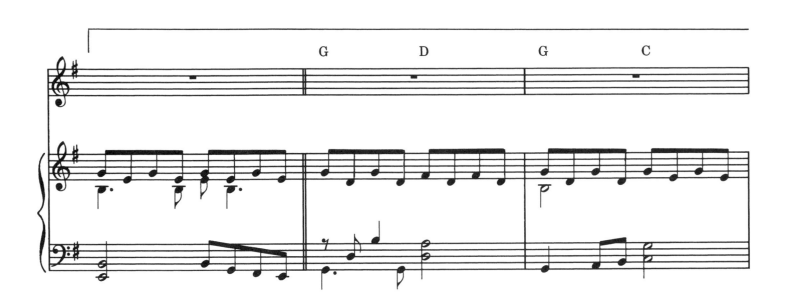

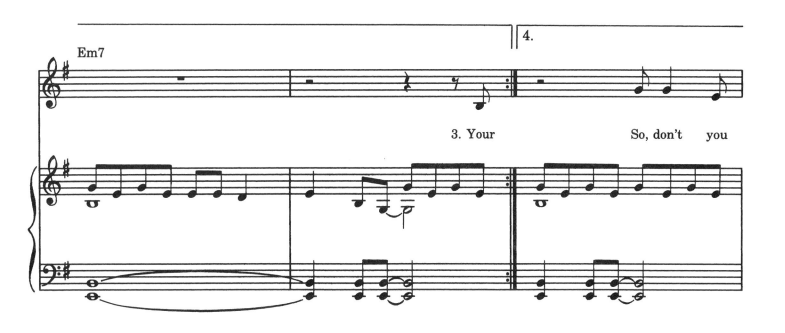

Verse 2:
Your mother she's an heiress, own's a block in St. John's Wood.
And your father'd be there with her if he only could.
To Chorus:

Verse 3:
Your old man took her diamonds and tiaras by the score.
Now she gets her kicks in Stepney, not in Knightsbridge any more.
To Chorus:

Verse 4:
Now, you've got some diamonds and you will have some others,
But you'd better watch your step girl or start living with your mother.
To Chorus:

RUBY TUESDAY

Words and Music by
MICK JAGGER and KEITH RICHARDS

THE SPIDER AND THE FLY

Words and Music by
MICK JAGGER and KEITH RICHARDS

Sit-tin' think-in' sink-in' drink-in' won - d'ring what I'ddo— when I'm

thru— to - night.— Smok-ing, mop-ing, may-be just hop-in'

188

When you're done you should go to bed.___

Don't say Hi,___ like the

spi - der to a fly. Jump right a - head and you're dead."___

*Guitar solo 1st time
Harmonica solo 2nd time

Coda

*8va if played by guitar

She was

Verse 2:
Sit up, fed up, low down, go 'round down to the bar at the place I'm at.
Sitting, drinking, superfic'ly thinking about the rinsed-out blonde on my left,
Then I said "Hi" like a spider to a fly,
Remembering what my little girl said.
To Guitar Solo

Verse 3:
She was common, flirty, she looked about thirty.
I would have run away but I was on my own.
She told me later, she's a machine operator,
She said she liked the way I held the microphone.
I said "My, My," like the spider to the fly,
"Jump right ahead in my web."
To Harmonica Solo

SAD DAY

Words and Music by
MICK JAGGER and KEITH RICHARDS

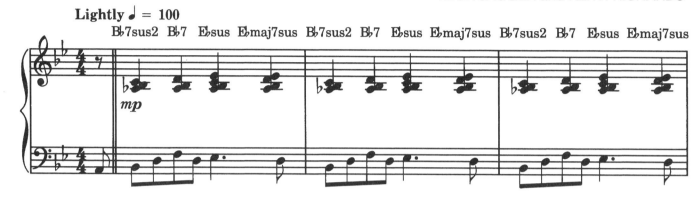

1. Some-one woke me up this morn - in' and I
(2.) called you on the phone __ and your
(3.) times that we had rows, __ but we

lit a cig - a - rette. __ Found my - self when I stopped yawn -
friend said, "She's _ not home." __ So I told her where I'd be at __
patched them up _ some-how. __ Think of the times I tried to go, __

(I CAN'T GET NO) SATISFACTION

Words and Music by
MICK JAGGER and KEITH RICHARDS

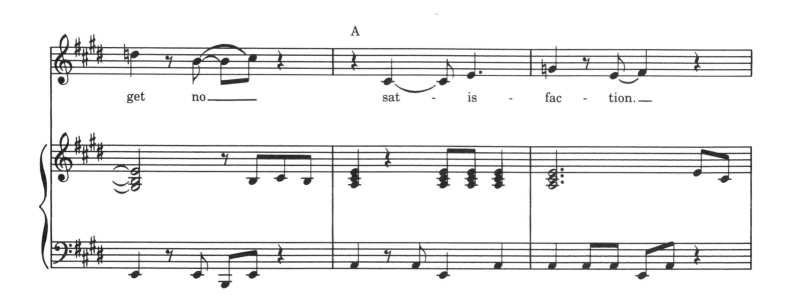

Verse 2:
When I'm watchin' my TV
And a man comes on and tells me
How white my shirts can be.
But, he can't be a man
'Cause he doesn't smoke the same cigarettes as me.

Verse 3:
When I'm ridin' 'round the world,
And I'm doin' this and I'm signin' that;
And I'm tryin' to make some girl,
Who tells me, baby, better come back maybe next week.
'Cause you see I'm on a losing streak.

SHE'S A RAINBOW

Words and Music by
MICK JAGGER and KEITH RICHARDS

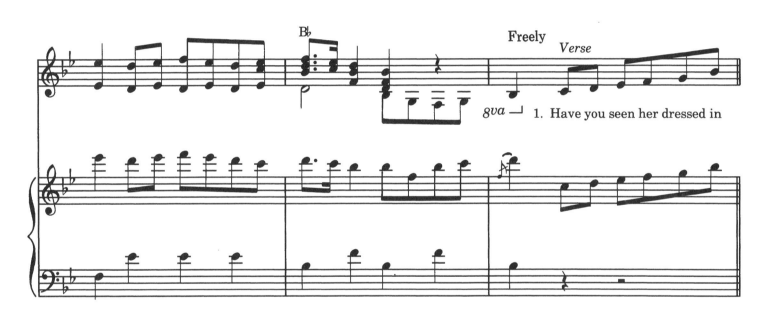

Freely

Verse

8va ⏌   1. Have you seen her dressed in

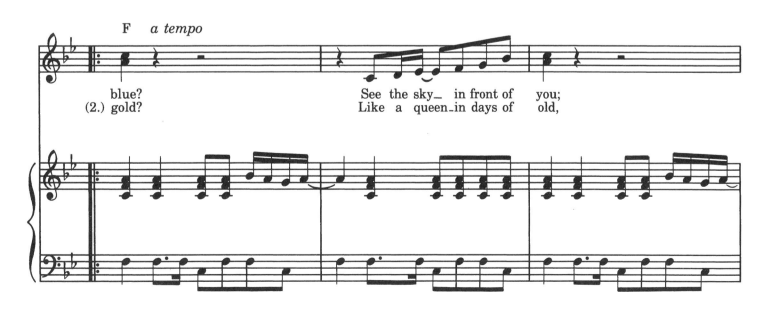

blue?

(2.) gold?

See the sky— in front of you;

Like a queen—in days of old,

and her face is like a sail, speck of white so fair and pale.
She shoots her col-ors all a-round like a sun-set go-ing down. } Have you seen a la-dy

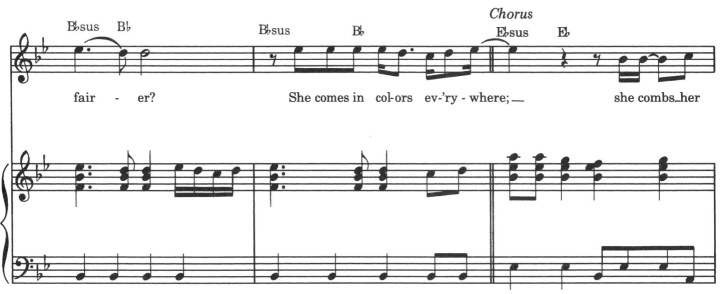

fair - er? She comes in col-ors ev'-ry - where;— she combs her

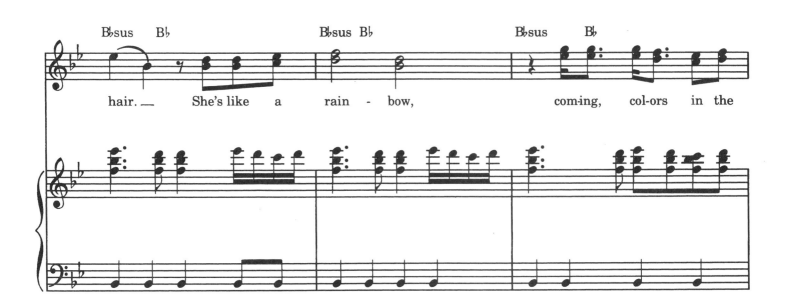

hair.— She's like a rain - bow, com-ing, col-ors in the

THE SINGER NOT THE SONG

Words and Music by
MICK JAGGER and KEITH RICHARDS

*8va if played by Guitar.

Verse 2:
It's not the way you give in willingly;
Others do it without thrilling me.
Giving me that same old...
To Chorus:

Verse 3:
The same old places and the same old songs,
We've been going there for much too long.
There's something wrong and it gives me that...
To Chorus:

STONED

Words and Music by
NANKER PHELGE

G7 *(Guitar first time only)**

out of my mind.

C7

G7

D7   C7

G7

1.

Here I go
Where am I at?

2. G7 (Pno.)

**8va if played by guitar.*

STREET FIGHTING MAN

Words and Music by
MICK JAGGER and KEITH RICHARDS

*Chords in parentheses for 2nd Verse.

I'll shout and scream, I'll kill the King, I'll rail

D. S. 𝄋 al Coda

at all his ser - vants. Well, then what

Coda

No!

(Guitar solo)*

*8va if played by guitar

Repeat ad lib. and fade

SURPRISE, SURPRISE

Words and Music by
MICK JAGGER and KEITH RICHARDS

To Coda

I could see it in your eyes.

guitar solo:

SYMPHATHY FOR THE DEVIL

Words and Music by
MICK JAGGER and KEITH RICHARDS

*8va if played by Guitar

Pleased to meet _you _

hope you guess _my name.   But what's con-

Lu-ci-fer__ 'cause I'm in need__ of some re - straint.__ So if you

meet me, have some__ cour - te-sy__ have some sym-pa-thy__ and some

taste. Use all your well__learned pol-i-tesse __ or I'll

lay your soul to waste.__

Pleased to meet— you ———— hope you guess—my name.

But what's puz-zling you — is the na-ture of— my

game.

Repeat ad lib. and fade

STUPID GIRL

Words and Music by
MICK JAGGER and KEITH RICHARDS

*8va if played by guitar

TRY A LITTLE HARDER

Words and Music by
MICK JAGGER and KEITH RICHARDS

TELL ME (YOU'RE COMING BACK TO ME)

Words and Music by
MICK JAGGER and KEITH RICHARDS

But this___ time it's dif-f'rent ___ dar - ling you'll see.
This time you're dif-f'rent ___ and de-ter-mined to go. You got-ta
I hear the tel-e - phone___ that has - n't rung.___

Chorus:

tell me you're com-ing back to me. You got - ta tell me you're com-ing

back to me. You got - ta tell me you're com-ing back to me. You got - ta

tell me you're com - ing back to me. back to me. You got - ta

TIME IS ON MY SIDE

Words and Music by
JERRY RAGOVOY

1. 2. 3. Time_____ is on my____ side.__ (Yes, it is.)

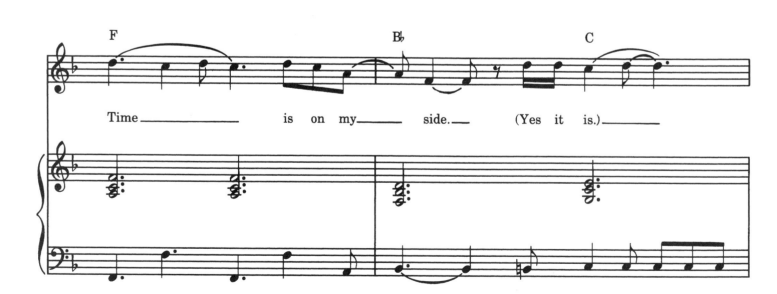

Time_____ is on my____ side.__ (Yes it is.)_____

246

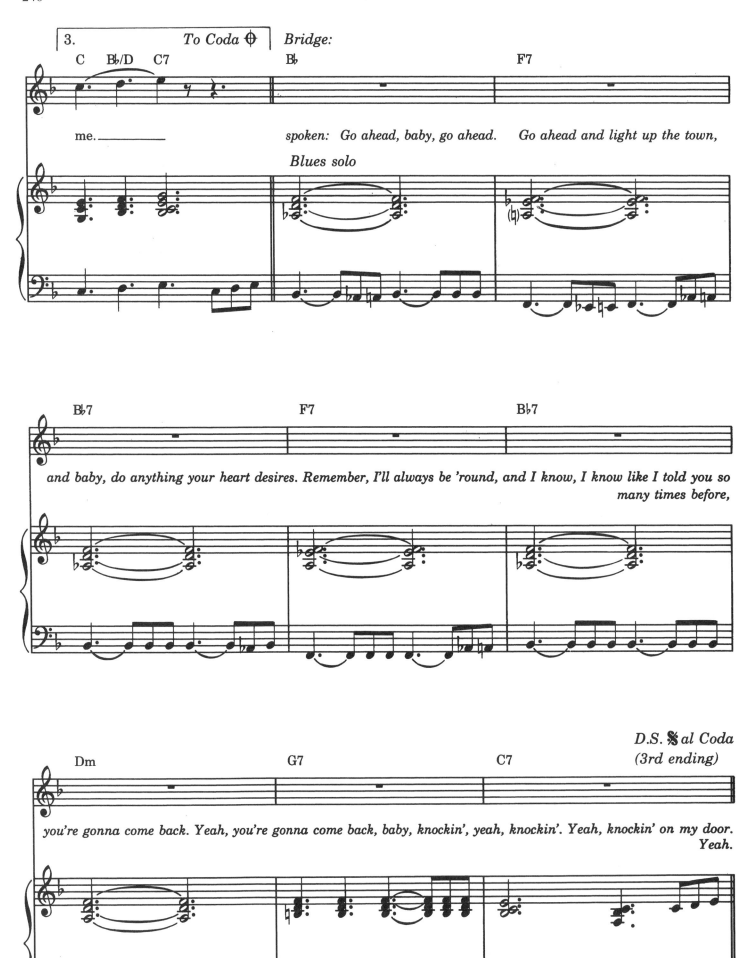

Time, time, time is on my ____ side. ____ (Yes it is.)_____

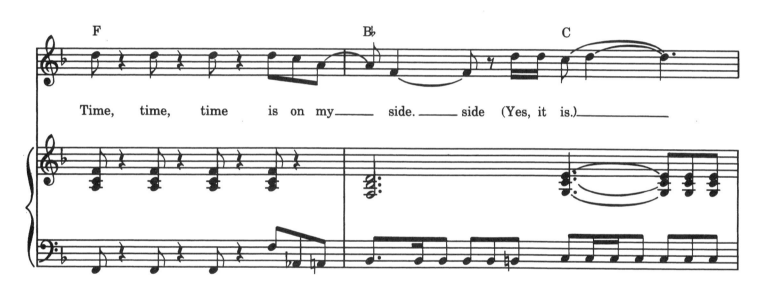

Time, time, time is on my ____ side. ____ side (Yes, it is.)_____

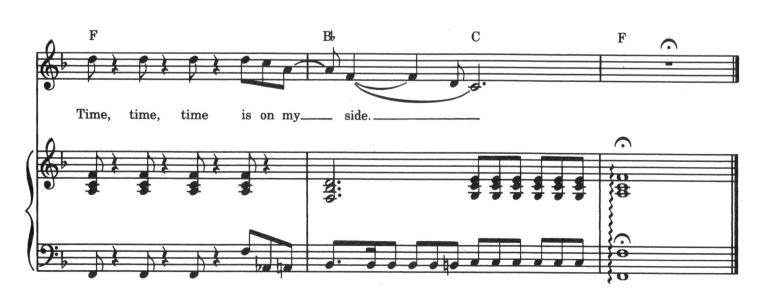

Time, time, time is on my ____ side._____

2000 LIGHT YEARS FROM HOME

Words and Music by
MICK JAGGER and KEITH RICHARDS

1. Sun turn - in' 'round with grace - ful mo - tion;
2. Bell flight four - teen you now can land;

250

Chorus:

It's   so

Outer space sound effects:

N.C.

a tempo

D. S. 𝄋 al Coda

R.H.

Coda

G   A

It's   so   ver - y lone - ly,   you're two thou - sand

light - years__ from home.

rit.

THE UNDER ASSISTANT WEST COAST PROMOTION MAN

Words and Music by
MICK JAGGER and KEITH RICHARDS

1. Harmonica solo (written)
2. Guitar solo
3. Vocal ad lib. to fade

Verse 2:
Well, I'm sittin' here thinkin' just how sharp I am.
Well, I'm sittin' here thinkin' just how sharp I am.
I'm an under assistant West Coast Promo man.
(To Harmonica Solo)

Verse 3:
Well, I promo groups when they come into town.
Well, I promo groups when they come into town.
Well, they laugh at my toupee, they're sure to put me down.
(To Guitar Solo)

Verse 4:
Well, I'm sittin' here thinkin' just how sharp I am.
Well, I'm sittin' here thinkin' just how sharp I am.
I'm a necessary talent behind ev'ry rock and roll band.
I'm sharp . . . *(ad lib.)*
(To Fade)

WE LOVE YOU

Words and Music by
MICK JAGGER and KEITH RICHARDS

love_____ you, we love _____ you.

You will nev-er win_ "we," your u-ni-forms_ don't fit "we." We for-

get the place_ we're in, 'cause_ we love_____ you. We

*8va if played by Guitar.

WHAT A SHAME

Words and Music by
MICK JAGGER and KEITH RICHARDS

*8va if played by guitar

*8va if played by guitar

D.S. 𝄋 *and fade (Harmonica solo)*

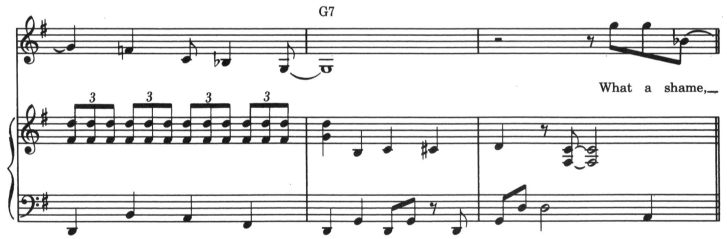

What a shame,__

Verse 2:
What a shame, they always wanna start a fight.
What a shame, always wanna start a fight.
Well, it scares me so I could sleep in a shelter all night.

Verse 3:
What a shame, ya all heard what I said.
What a shame, ya all heard what I said.
Ya might wake up in the morning and find your poor self dead.

WHO'S DRIVING YOUR PLANE?

Words and Music by
MICK JAGGER and KEITH RICHARDS

*8va if played by guitar.

Verse:

1. It was your fa-ther who trained you and your moth-er who brained you to

be so use - less and shy.___ But I just re - placed them and tried___

___ not to break them___ be-cause you could stand up___ if you tried.___ And I, I

274

WILD HORSES

Words and Music by
MICK JAGGER and KEITH RICHARDS

Moderately slow ♩ = 88

*Lead guitar:

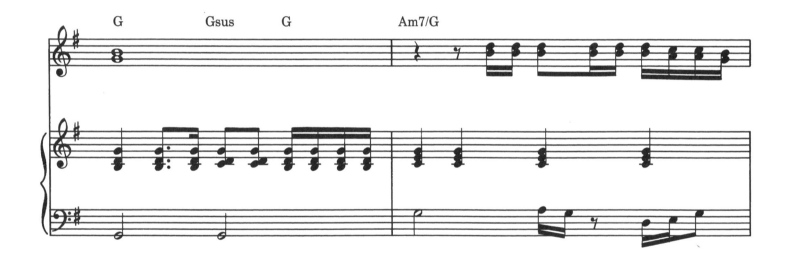

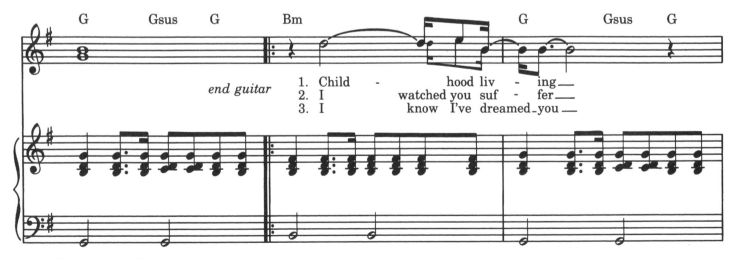

1. Child - hood liv - ing
2. I watched you suf - fer
3. I know I've dreamed you

end guitar

* *8va if played by Guitar.*

* 8va if played by Guitar.

* 8va if played by Guitar.

YOU CAN'T ALWAYS GET WHAT YOU WANT

Words and Music by
MICK JAGGER and KEITH RICHARDS

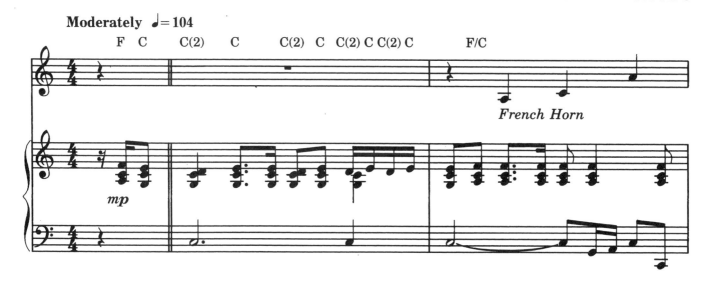

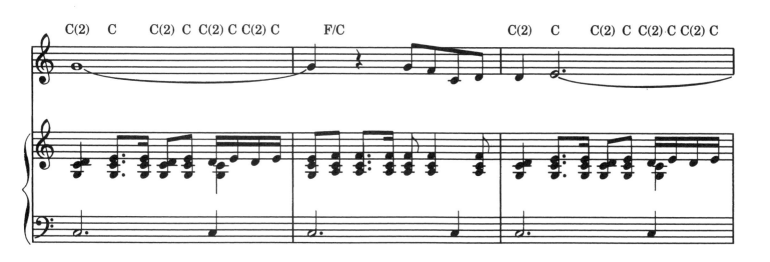

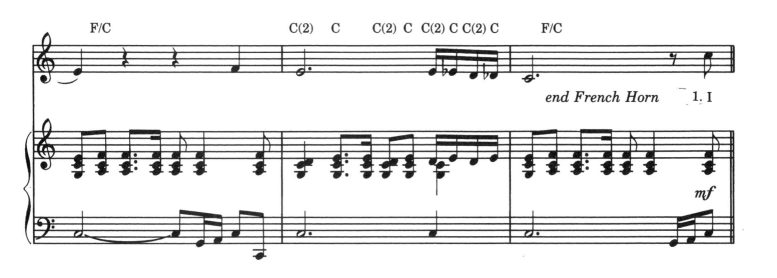

try some-times, you just might find,_ you just might find_____ you get what you

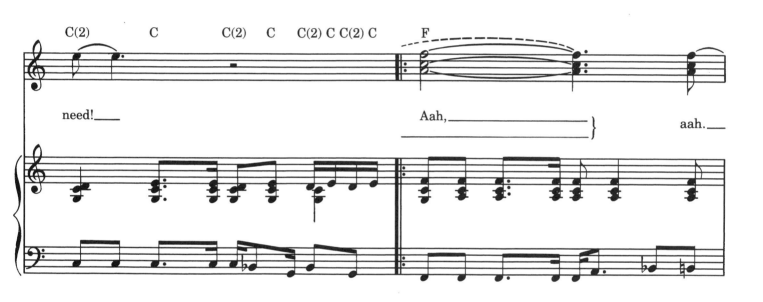

need!___

Aah,_____ } aah.___

Repeat ad lib. and fade

_____

Aah_____

The Rolling Stones

Songbooks for Musicians and Collectors

Available everywhere books and musical instruments are sold!

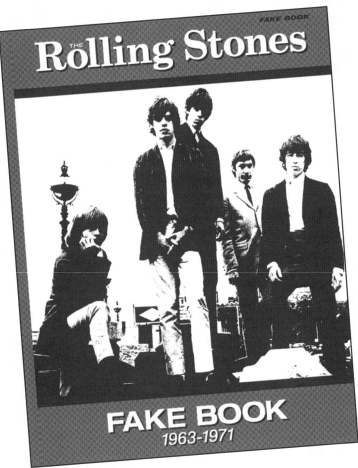

For All Musicians

The most comprehensive Rolling Stones songbook ever produced! A beautiful collectible that features full-color vintage sheet music artwork and over 400 pages of "fakebook"-style charts for 167 Rolling Stones songs from the band's dynamic 1963–1971 period. Includes complete lyrics and melodies, chords changes, and selected note-for-note TAB transcriptions of essential guitar riffs and solos— the perfect gift for any Rolling Stones fan.

FBM0008 The Rolling Stones Fake Book 1963–1971

For Pianists and Keyboardists

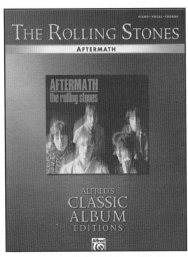

25775 Aftermath (Piano/Vocal edition)

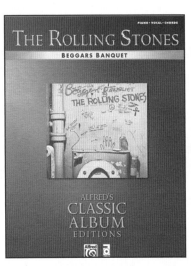

25773 Beggars Banquet (Piano/Vocal edition)

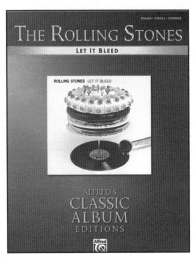

25737 Let It Bleed (Piano/Vocal edition)